how to
heal
the hurt
by hating

how to heal the hurt by hating

Anita Liberty

Ballantine Books • New York

A Ballantine Book
Published by The Ballantine Publishing Group

Published in the United States by
The Ballantine Publishing Group,
a division of Random House, Inc., New York,
and simultaneously in
Canada by Random House of Canada Limited, Toronto.

http://www.randomhouse.com

Library of Congress Cataloging-in-Publication Data

Liberty, Anita.
How to heal the hurt by hating / Anita Liberty. — 1st ed.
p.   cm.
ISBN 0-345-42374-7 (alk. paper)
1. Man–woman relationships—Poetry.   2. Separation (Psychology)—
Poetry.   3. Man–woman relationships—Humor.   4. Separation
(Psychology)—Humor.   5. Revenge—Poetry.   6. Revenge—Humor.
I. Title.
PS3562.I213H69   1998
811'.54—dc21   98-19072
                                                                CIP

Text and cover design by Michael Calleia/Industrial Strength Design

Manufactured in the United States of America

First Edition: September 1998

10 9 8 7 6 5 4 3 2 1

For Mitchell.

Hi Mitchell.
You were a **big jerk**
and now everybody knows it.

happy
to be
alive

For Mitchell Love Liberty
A poem I wrote three and a half years ago

Oh, I'm happy.
Happy.
Happy to be alive.
Glad.
Overjoyed.
Delighted.
I'm in ecstasy
just about all of the time.
I can barely remember
what being angry felt like.
Flowers bloom.
Birds sing.
Sun shines.
And love poems get written.
At first I thought it
was the caffeine in my coffee,
but it was decaf.
I checked.
Then I blamed my hormones,
but it was the week before my period.
The week before my period.
I don't think I've ever been happy.
But if I have,
I've certainly never been happy
during the week before my period.
Why? Why?
A man makes me happy.
There, I wrote it.
There's no taking it back.
His name is Mitchell
and because of him,
angels dance,
rivers flow,
fireworks explode,
and an angry poet loses her edge.

big mistake

big mistake

i hate him i hate him i hate him i hate him
i hate him i hate him i hate him i hate him
i hate him i hate him i hate him i hate him
i hate him i hate him i hate him i hate him
i hate him i hate him i hate him i hate him
i hate him i hate him i hate him i hate him
i hate him i hate him i hate him i hate him
i hate him i hate him i hate him i hate him
i hate him i hate him i hate him i hate him
i hate him i hate him i hate him i hate him
i hate him i hate him i hate him i hate him
i hate him i hate him i hate him i hate him
i hate him i hate him i hate him i hate him
i hate him i hate him i hate him i hate him
i hate him i hate him i hate him i hate him
i hate him i hate him i hate him i hate him
i hate him i hate him i hate him i hate him
i hate him i hate him i hate him i hate him
i hate him i hate him i hate him i hate him
i hate him i hate him i hate him i hate him

Lizzy and Samantha came over tonight. They had
to. Mitchell left me yesterday because he's IN LOVE
WITH SOMEONE ELSE. And **Party of Five** was on. God, I
adore that show. At this point, it's the only thing
that makes me want to keep living. That, and my drive
to make Mitchell pay for this huge tear in my otherwise seamless ego. Fixing this one is going to be a lot
of work and very expensive. He broke it, he bought it.
Anyway, Liz and Sam come over and order Chinese food
and watch **Fiesta de Cinco** and I walk around the
apartment holding a black Hefty trash bag with a
white sticker on the side to identify that which
holds: THINGS THAT BELONG TO MITCHELL. I put in
everything THAT BELONGS TO MITCHELL in the apartment
that we shared. At a commercial break in **La Fiesta**,
Liz stated (with her mouth full of her last bite of
scallion pancake), "Whatever you want, take it now."
I didn't question her judgment. She'd been through
a number of break-ups in the past and, besides, she
was probably thinking more clearly than I was at
the moment.

What I Took:
1. His Elvis Costello CD (**Brutal Youth**)
2. Framed photographs I'd given him of the trip to
   Nova Scotia we took WHEN WE WERE HAPPY
3. The hypoallergenic pillow I bought for him JUST
   BECAUSE I CARED
4. The softest white shirt from the GAP that had been
   my present to him JUST LAST WEEK WHILE, I GUESS I
   REALIZE NOW, HE WAS BUSILY PLOTTING HOW HE WOULD
   LEAVE ME FOR ANOTHER WOMAN
5. The flannel shirt of his that I always used to
   borrow...now, it's mine

I gave Samantha the green linen shirt he gave
me for my birthday last year. I liked it at the time.
I don't like it now. Liz offered to keep everything
for me at her place until I was ready to take it back.
I can't imagine when that will be. I don't even want
those things. I just don't want HIM to have them.

He seems to have scurried away with the bare essentials: toothbrush, razor, a couple of shirts, jeans, underwear and the book he's in the middle of reading: his dog-eared copy of **Darkness Visible** by William Styron. That should have been a sign. So even though he left most of his belongings behind, it took me only six minutes to consolidate them into one garbage bag.

His life = One garbage bag.

There's a little justice in that.

If your lover starts reading William Styron's
Darkness Visible: A Memoir of Madness
(in case you're unfamiliar with the book,
it's a true account of Styron's descent into
clinical and chronic depression), there
may be a problem. There may not,
but there may be. You just might want
to check in and see if everything's okay.
It may be a sign.

promises

{ Promises can be broken.
Promises were made to be broken.
Your promises mean nothing. }

What? I'm just giving you examples
of how to use the goddamned word
in a fucking sentence.

You meet someone.
He seems great. Warm. Attentive. Smart. Cute.
But…he has a girlfriend.
Don't do it. Just don't.
Stop yourself. You can do that.
You don't throw yourself in front of trains.
You can act rationally. You've done it before.
He has a girlfriend.
She could be you. You could be her.
And sure you're incredible.
But he thought I was, too, when he met me.
I mean, let me try that again…he thought *she* was, too, when he met *her*.
And he made a commitment to *her*. A commitment he was willing to break.
You do the math.

Samantha once asked me which experience I
thought would be scarier: seeing a ghost or being
abducted by aliens. Here's my answer: Neither. Nothing
could ever be as terrifying as finding myself at the
same party as Mitchell and his new girlfriend. Since
that happened last night, I guess I can live the rest
of my life without fear.

Mitchell's New Girlfriend
A Poem in Five Parts

1 Her name is Heather.

2 She skis.
She climbs mountains.
She goes white water rafting.
She even owns her very own pair of
rollerblades.
I'm so happy for her.
Really. I am.

3 Mitchell and Heather.
Mitchell and Heather.
Mitchell and Heather.
Big fucking deal.

4 Hmm. Given a choice…
What would I rather be good at?
Windsurfing or the honest and noble
expression of my artistic impulse?
Hmm.

5 Heather.
A woman.
Like me.
Not like me.
Poor Heather.
Not like me.
Because now Mitchell's *her* problem.
Poor Heather.

You are wrong.

You always were.

I am right.

I always have been.

Who's sorry now?

Answer the question.

Mitchell broke my heart.

So I broke his
marble cof

fee table.

   I have a problem with commitment, so I decided
to become a temp. I got called in for a job today,
answering phones. I was so bored that I tried to move
a pen with my mind. And then my temp agency called to
make sure I had shown up on time (I had) and was wearing "corporate attire" (I wasn't). The other line rang
while I was on the first call and as I tried to find
the Hold button, the second line stopped ringing. I got
off the phone with the temp agency and started to
think about lunch (it was 9:15 A.M.). I heard the click
of a door behind me and I turned around to suffer the
steely-eyed look of a woman who has no life. "Were you
on the phone?" she asked me. "I am not an idiot! I
spend my days thinking large thoughts and wrestling
with issues of impurity and complexity and trying to
unclog the drain of my creativity while I roam aimful-
ly on the chaotic fringes of a society on which I doubt
we can agree!" That's what I **wanted** to say. What I **said**
was: "Yes, is that a problem?" To which she responded,
"Well, I had to pick up the other line." "Oh, **you** had to
pick up the other line. Come here, please, so I can
sink my nails into the sagging flesh of your inexpres-
sive face. I know what you're thinking. Blame the temp.
Blame the temp. She's only in it for the money. She
won't remember us. And she won't be here tomorrow."

Never went outside today. Didn't clean my apartment. Didn't shower. Didn't write. Didn't watch television. The phone didn't ring. Not once. I didn't get any mail. Oh. That's not true. I got a Chinese menu. **Someone** was thinking about me. But I didn't order anything. I ate chips. Drank soda. And I'm so confident, I don't feel **bad** about my day. I feel empowered. At the end of a day like that, any average person might feel like a failure, like a loser, like a completely unpopular, unmotivated, immobilized lump sitting on an old futon. I don't. I don't. Do not. Don't. DON'T. Shut up. I'm going to bed.

Slipping slowly, deeply,
down the drain of my life.
Consumed by the darkness
of my unfulfilled dreams.

Black heat surrounds my lonely —

oh, desperately lonely — body.

My existence has become

a blur of dissatisfaction and I

feel nothing but what I don't have

and that is everything.

Don't feel bad —

I mean, it's not like it's your fault or anything.

Oh yeah, actually, it is.

My sister is getting married this summer. My younger sister. I don't really care. Really I don't. I mean why would I want to be tied down to one person when it's so much fun to date?

ADVICE FROM **ANITA LIBERTY**

When your self-esteem is low,
do not call someone who has rejected you in the past.
The chance that that person will say something
that will make you feel worse is great.
The chance that that person will say exactly
what it is that you need to hear is slim.

Just because I give advice doesn't mean I follow it.

**You're a bad habit.
I want to kick you...**

Smile

Walking down the New York City street;
with my face twisted into a gargoyle grimace
as a warning to all those
who might cross my path.

I'm not lost in my thoughts;
I know exactly where I'm going.

And thus I see him only when he speaks to me.

"Cheer up, baby. It can't be that bad!"

Oh, it can't, can it?

Well, have a fucking seat and let me tell you exactly how
bad it can be:

First of all, I'm on my way to
some demeaning temp job for which I have to wear
"professional attire."

The subway ride to midtown during **rush hour**
always gives me a lift.

My boyfriend left me for a woman named **Heather.**

My parents still feel justified in treating me like an
eleven-year-old.

There was just a little **too much latte** in my latte.

My sister is getting married. **MY YOUNGER SISTER!**

I'm **obsessed** with my own mortality.

And I am constantly having to fend off
people like you who seem to flock to me
as if you had been beckoned.

"Lighten up."
"Be happy."
"Why the frown?"
"Smile! It's a beautiful day!"

Oh shut up.

I worked hard to find the darkest mood I could.
I won't give it up that easy.
And you—you with your
    cheer-ups
smiles
    behappies
you just gave me another reason to stay there.

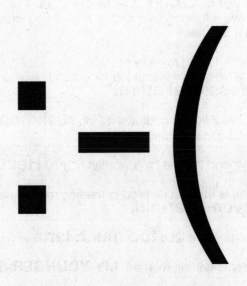

A Visit to the Gynecologist

At the gynecologist's office
fearing the inevitable...
questions.
"Are you still with the same boyfriend?"
　"No."
"Do you have a new boyfriend?"
　"No."
"Have you been sexually active since your
last visit?"
　"Um, yes."
"With more than one partner?"
　"Oh, you mean, sexually active with a partner?
　Well, then, no, I guess I haven't been sexually active
　since my last visit."
And then no more words are exchanged.
The facts are recorded on my chart.
　Name: Anita Liberty
　Weight: 100 pounds.
　Date of last period: The 5th
　Status: Alone. Not getting any.
　　　　Hasn't in a long time.
And so I stare up at the fluorescent light
on my doctor's ceiling,
as she makes idle chit-chat.
She's up to her elbow in me
and my mind tells my body,
"No, Mitchell's not back.
This is Dr. Harris,
and she hasn't got time for what you want.
Got it?"
But Dr. Harris does tell me I have a beautiful vagina
and I will hold onto that compliment for days as a
shipwrecked survivor
　　　　　clings
　　　　　　　to
　　　　　　　　a piece
　　　　　　　　　　of driftwood.

I know. I know. I know what today is, thank you.
I got flowers. From my mother. I got chocolate. From my
father. I got a phone call. From Lizzy. I got a card.
From my sister and her fiancé. Charming. They all
want to be my valentine. Yeah, right. Being my valentine means one thing and one thing only. And no one
who's related to you should be offering to do that one
thing for you. Okay. I'm loved. But not romantically.
Familial love and friendship just don't cut it on a
day like today. Would having dinner with my parents
on Valentine's Day be worse than spending it alone?
Tough call. I went down to the basement of my building
to find a box of valentines from boyfriends past and
found them half-eaten by maggots. Maggots! The box con-
taining them had fallen to the damp, dirt floor and
the little critters had had a feast on those flimsy,
two-dimensional representations of what (in every case)
turned out to be short-term devotion. If Valentine's
Day is for lovers, leave the rest of us out of it.

he told me that i'm beautiful when i'm angry. **big mistake**

So I have to move. Move out of the apartment that I found for me and Mitchell to live in. I have to move. I can't stay here. Even though I've successfully removed every trace of the weasel, it's still **our** place. Moving is never easy. And moving when you have to is even harder. But fortunately, I got the help I needed. Their names were Herb and Luis. I wrote them an ode:

----->

The Men Who Moved Me

Herb and Luis
are the men who moved me.

I am not easy to move.
I admit it.
But Herb and Luis
were not intimidated.
They accepted the challenge.
They're professionals.

They took everything I hold precious
and treated it with care.
(Sound familiar?
I didn't think so.)
Each photograph,
each floppy disk,
every book,
letter and dying plant
held surely in their arms.
They made sure nothing
(and nobody)
got hurt.
They told me it would be okay
and it was.
I was moved.
No, more like transported.
And as quickly as they came into my life
they were gone.
Because that's how I wanted it.

Herb and Luis.
I've never been moved by men
quite the way I was moved by them.
Men who picked me up and
didn't let me down
until I told them to.

Why must the city be so unkind?
What did I ever do to it?
Why must it punish me for
being single?
Why must I pay twice as much
for an apartment twice as small
as those of my friends living in
the blissful state of cohabitation?

Less money.
More room.
And sex.

Just one of those.
I'd take just one of those.

But instead,
I am confined to a studio
with a rent I can't afford
in bed alone
in my sleeping alcove
and watching cable TV —
a thirty-one dollar and forty-two cent a
    month luxury
that I have to pay for
all by myself,
as long as I am
all by myself.

Why must the city be so unkind?

EXCERPT FROM **ANITA LIBERTY'S DIARY**

I didn't have a temp job today. In fact, I had
nothing to do today at all. Nothing. But I'm a writer. A
poet. I had the whole day to stay home and write poetry. So what did I do? I got a big cup of coffee, turned
on my computer, and played one game of solitaire. Or
what I thought would be one game of solitaire. Six
hours later and I still hadn't written a thing. But
I did win 7 out of 245 games of solitaire.
What a day.

I wish we were back together
For just one night
So I could --

push you out of my loftbed
while you were sleeping.

Temp job. It was in midtown. Hellish. Truly. I realized something today when I was in the elevator of this huge office building: chivalry is not dead. Far from it, much to my dismay. In crowded midtown office building elevators, male passengers insist on stepping aside to let female passengers off first. No matter if all the men are in the front of the elevator. No matter if the elevator is so crowded that there's no room to step aside. No matter if stepping aside means that it takes all of us twice as long to get out the door. Well, I'd like to take the liberty of speaking for my gender when I say, "Just get off the goddamned elevator, you idiots! Just get off. Don't worry about me. Don't even think about me. When the doors open, just get out. Get out. You have one thing to remember and one thing only: Elevator stops. Doors open. Get the fuck out of my way."

Lizzy called and woke me up this morning.
Someone has to. She said that she was out with
some people last night who know Heather (Mitchell's
new girlfriend, for those of you who have not been
paying attention). They told her that Heather isn't
funny. They told her that, in fact, Heather actually
thinks she's funny, but she's not. That is the worst
combination of things I could possibly imagine.
A small victory. But I'll take it.

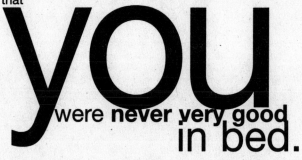

Now that you're **gone and never coming back**, I feel that I can be **honest** about the fact that **you** were **never very good** in bed.

He won't be different.
Only better.

Better-looking,
better in bed,
better for me,
better than you.

And I won't be different.

Only better.
off without you.

Make him pay for your sins.

And then tell him where you live.

Motherhood eludes me. That is, until I go to sleep
at night. Then, all of a sudden...I'm pregnant, I give
birth (usually Michael J. Fox is in the delivery room), I
change diapers, I nurse. Of course, it's not always a
human baby. Sometimes it's a puppy, or a piglet, or a
cat. But it's always mine. And I always love it. But as
my **body** creates these dreams of motherhood -- the
healthy, satisfying, uncomplicated part of motherhood --
my **mind** puts in the panic-stricken, failing, desperate,
emotionally-overburdened part of motherhood.

And dreams turn to nightmares. The piglet runs away.
The puppy has two heads. The mutation won't eat. I for-
get I have it so I forget to take care of it.
I make mistakes.
I can't fulfill its needs.
I don't know what it wants from me.
It becomes the source of anxiety.
It becomes something I'm not good at.
I usually wake up screaming.

Once I am awake, I am comforted by the sight of my
unpregnant belly, and I breathe the inevitable sigh
of relief. Only the slightest regret creeps into my
consciousness -- I gave birth to a very cute piglet.

How Old Am I?
by Anita Liberty, age 6

How old am **I**?

How old am **I**?

I am **six.**

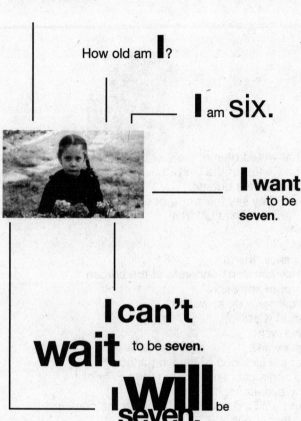

I want to be **seven.**

I can't wait to be **seven.**

I **will** be **seven.**

The Center of the Universe
by Anita Liberty, age 13

That would be me.
The Center of the Universe.
No one here but me.
And They say the world doesn't revolve
    around Anita Liberty!
HA!
HA!
I'll show them.
They just don't understand the burden
    of my position.
It carries a lot of weight.
And I wait…
and wait…
and wait…
for the lifeblood of my womanhood
to begin coursing through the cavity of
my ever-changing body…
And until it does, I am caught in the purgatory
    that is puberty.
And They act as if everything's completely normal.
They ask me, "How was the math test?"
As if I care about the math test.
They ask me, "How's school?" as if that question doesn't
    send a burning spear through the soft palate of my
    adolescence.
They ask me "What's new?"
As if I could explain the constantly evolving reality of my
    own desperate existence.
They ask me, "Why are you so irritable all the time?"

As if I could suppress the persistent anger that
feeds off of the convention of our nuclear family.
They don't understand that I was put here for a higher
purpose.
Don't ask me any questions…
about anything.
Don't expect me to be polite…
to anyone.
Don't look at me…
not even a glance in my direction.

Or I just
might lose
it.

captious

{ You want to know what it means?

Look it up. }

EXCERPT FROM **ANITA LIBERTY'S DIARY**

Felt kind of depressed today. Gee. I wonder why. So I called a friend from college who I hadn't talked to in a while. Cheryl. She's married. My married friends freak me out a little bit. They get married and all of a sudden their husbands are their best friends and they have all kinds of secrets that they can't tell you and you wouldn't understand because you're not married. Then when you call, they make you talk to their husbands when you only called to talk to them. They start talking about having babies when you call to talk about yourself. They start trying to have babies. That's all they talk about, how much sex they have to have and when. Like I need to hear about that. And then, God forbid, it works and they get pregnant. That's all they talk about. They have the baby. That's all they talk about. Then, when you call, you have to talk to their husbands and their infant children and when you finally have them on the phone, alone, they have to go because their husbands just got home
or the baby just got up
or the baby needs to be fed
or the baby did something cute.

Not that cute.

I have

no
- graduate degree,
- important job,
- car,
- mortgage,
- diamond ring,
- husband,
- babies,
- boyfriend.

So?
I've done plenty in the past decade.
I have.
Let's see…

I have
received **two** diplomas,
been hired **five** times,
quit **four** times,
been fired **once**
        (one of my proudest
        accomplishments),
lived in **three** states,
had **six** apartments,
been to small claims court **once**
        (but I'm looking forward
        to going back),
had **five** boyfriends,
been in love **once** (maybe **twice**),
given birth to over a **hundred** poems,
had all **four** wisdom teeth removed,
and I have been a blonde,
        a **brunette,**
        and a redhead.

Time has **not** been wasted.

Quite the opposite, in fact.

While my peers have been

blindly falling off the cliff

like

lemmings

pushed

by

society's

hand,

I

have been living my life as   only I can live it:

Disappointing the
expectations of
others.

Ten-Day Countdown
An Emotional Chronicle of the Ten Days Before My Thirtieth Birthday

Ten days before:
> Don't know.

Nine days before:
> Ambivalent.

Eight days before:
> Slightly anxious, but mostly confident.

Seven days before:
> All right already. Let's get this thing over with. I'm tired of waiting to see how it all turns out. Bring my thirties on. I'm ready for 'em.

Six days before:
> Oh God, I have less than a week left in my twenties.

Five days before:
> Thank God I have less than a week left in my twenties.

Four days before:
> I never thought I'd still look this hot at 30.

Three days before:
> Don't know.

Two days before:
> So. That's it. I'm not going to have a baby by the time I'm 30. Fine. Didn't want one anyway. Who ever said I did?

The day before:
> Hey...I completely forgot about presents.
> I love presents.

Today I Am 30

Today I am **30**.
I am not depressed.
I am not indifferent.
I am not depressed.
Why would I be depressed?
Because you expect me to be?
All the more reason not to be.

Today I am **30**.
Finally.
Finally.

30 is my ticket.
30 is what I've been waiting for.
30 is a cloak of confidence
I get to wear for the rest of my life.
The mettle with which I will
renew my fight against
social injustice and mass emotional indifference.
30 is the pair of 3-D glasses
that allows me to see
beyond the omnipresent
apathy of those who
surround me.
It's freedom.
It's legitimacy.
It's like getting your driver's license,
when you feel like you've
had a learner's permit forever.

30 is poetic license.
A license for me to speak directly.
Call it as I see it.
Who's going to stop me?
Today, I am **30**.

I'm not married.
I don't have a baby.
I hear no ticking clock.
I've been digital since 1984.
All of those things that I was supposed

to accomplish by the time I was **30**
are not accomplished.
So I no longer have to worry
about the agenda someone else handed to me.
I'm no longer on any agenda.

Today I am **30**
and the only responsibility I have
is myself.
My sanity.
My integrity.
My health.
My peace of mind.
My acute and unerring perceptions.
An enormous responsibility to be sure,
but mine and mine alone.
I am a fully responsible adult.
Because today I am **30**.

Not a bad place to be actually.
After all, how many people can say:
Today I am **30** and
today I am free.

EXCERPT FROM **ANITA LIBERTY'S DIARY**

My sister Hope's wedding shower was this after-
noon. Seemed to go pretty well. I had asked everyone
to dress up like a different time of day and night
and then bring a present that related to that time.
Some women came in nightgowns, some in robes, sweats,
exercise clothes, business suits, and little black
evening dresses. Each of them was wearing a tag that
had a time of day/night written on it, a time that cor-
responded to their outfits. I wore jeans and a t-shirt.
My time was "4:00 A.M." I'm an artist. Everything was
going fine until Alicia (my younger sister's friend
from work) asked me out loud, from across the room, in
front of everybody, while my sister was opening a present, "So, Anita, what's going on in your love life?
Any wedding bells ringing for you? Are you and that
guy...what was his name...Michael, Matthew,
Marvin...going to go for it?" "His name is Mitchell,"
I replied icily. "Oh, that's right, Mitchell. So are you
getting ready to follow in your younger sister's foot-
steps?" My sister tried unsuccessfully to intervene...
but I stopped her. "We broke up, Alicia. Mitchell and
I broke up." Alicia seemed appropriately sympathetic...
for a minute. "Oh, I'm so sorry to hear that." And then:
"And didn't you just turn thirty?" What circle of Hell
have I entered? "Yes, Alicia, I did just turn thirty."
"And you're not dating **anyone**?" "No, Alicia, I'm not
dating **anyone**." "Wow. That's got to be tough. Ooooh,
Hope, is that from Victoria's Secret? I love that." I'm
going to have to kill Alicia. Soon.

am the **Queen of Conflict**.
I wear a **crown of self-righteousness** upon my head.

I sit in the **throne of argument**
and am cloaked in the **robe of anger**.

I hold a **scepter** made of the finest **aggravation**
and live in the **Palace of Injustice**.

I rule in the **land of Wanna-Make-Something-Of-It?**
where it's always **that** time of the month.

I'm married to the **King of What's-Your-Problem?**
and the **Prince of Discord** is heir to the throne.

My subjects are **discontented and antagonistic**
and I **drown** those who cross me in the moat of contempt.

"Off with their heads," **I cry**.
"Let them eat cake," **I cry**.
"We are not amused," **I cry**.
"Long live me,"   I cry.

runs through my **Blue blood**

black heart.

The Queen of Conflict rules.

pride

{ I have to be proud, because if I weren't
you might think you're as good as I am
and that wouldn't be any fun for me at all. }

      Obviously, my answering machine does not
discriminate, because I came home to a message from
Mitchell.

Hey Anita. It's Mitchell. I'm just calling to say "Hi."

      Oh, thank you, Mitchell. You've made my life
complete.

It's Mitchell. I'm just calling to say "Hi."

      You can't fool me. You're not calling to say "Hi."
You're not calling to see how I am or calling to let
bygones be bygones. You're calling because you want
to be sure I haven't forgotten. No, I haven't forgotten.
How could I when your memory wakes me up every
morning at 6:00 A.M.?

I'm just calling to say "Hi."

      Call to say that you miss me. Call to say you've
made a mistake. Call to say you can't live without me.
But don't bother to call if you're:

Just calling to say "Hi."

      You must be:

"Hi."

Love

Love is not red roses.
Love is not a box of candy.
Love is not a perfumed letter.
Love is more like a blood-sucking leech that
attaches itself to you and drains you
of your common sense and dignity.

Love doesn't make you feel warm and fuzzy.
Love worms its way around your
insides infecting your body until
you are so diseased that others
aren't safe being in the same room with you.

Love is not a gentle breeze.
Love grabs you by the throat and
blows its hot air in your face until
you're dying of thirst
and your nostrils are on fire
and your contacts are really dry and uncomfortable.

Love is not patient.
Love interrupts you and cuts you off midsentence
because it thinks that what it's got to say is
more important.

Love is not my friend.
Love can take a long walk off a short pier.
Love can take a flying leap through a rolling donut.
Love can sit on this and rotate.

Love can eat me for a long time and like it.

People talk a lot about "letting go" — how that's the only way
you can truly get over a break-up and move on,
the only way to show your strength and exhibit growth.

Here's what I think about letting go:
You don't have to.

[*EXCERPT FROM TRANSCRIPT OF "OPEN MIKE NIGHT" AT THE POETRY CLUB, NEW YORK CITY, RECORDED LIVE ON MARCH 16, 1997*]

PERFORMER A

And thus concludes my tribute to Walt Whitman, a seven-voice, multi-media, performance event in progress. What you saw tonight was just thirty-five minutes of what I anticipate will become a seven-hour song cycle. Please feel free to approach me at the end of the evening with any and all criticisms, suggestions, and, of course, commendations. I thank you.

[*Scattered applause.*]

HOST

Thank you, Sean, for that...that...thank you for that. Now I bring you a complete novice to our stage here at The Poetry Club. Women and men: Anita Liberty!

[*Silence.*]

ANITA LIBERTY

Umm. Thank you. Good evening. I am Anita Liberty. The poem you are about to hear was written to sate the hunger in an artist's belly. That you are witness to it, that there is an audience at all is purely incidental. It's called "My Goal" and I dedicate it to my ex-boyfriend, Mitchell.

I will use my vision to be mean
and watch you sweat.
Shake a finger.
Recall sordid moments.
Say what I want.
Tell it like it was.
Rip away your suit.
Show you bare and weak.
It's my only dream.
No one can stop me.
I am mad and gorgeous.

[*Silence. A glass breaks. Someone coughs.*]

ANITA LIBERTY (cont'd.)

Thank you.

[*Anita Liberty leaves the stage. There is feedback from the microphone.*]

not thinking about you

Not Thinking About You

Not thinking about you.
Not thinking about you.
Still **not** thinking about you.

I do**n't** care what you're doing.
I do**n't** care who you're with.
Because I am **not** thinking about you.
You are occupying **no** part of my thoughts.

No sirree.
You are **not** on my mind.
I am **not** kidding.
I'm **not** even trying **not** to think about you.
I'm just **not** thinking about you.
At all.

I am **not** thinking…oops.
Wait a minute.
I did just have a thought about you.
No…I'm wrong…it was about someone else.

Still **not** thinking about you.
Not thinking about you.
No matter how hard I try,
I just can't stop **not** thinking about you.

truth

{ The truth is that I'm not thinking about Mitchell.
I don't care if you don't believe me.
It's the truth. }

Just another day. Just another temp job. I type
and I watch. I type and I listen. I sense I am an oddi-
ty to them. The men. You know, the men who run **everything**. And so I play with them. The men covered neck
to toe in suits of wool. (The current incarnation of the
wolf in sheep's clothing!) And I let them think I'm
innocent to their intentions. I let them sidle up to
me, flirting, bantering, strutting their wares in
front of me until I pull them close and whisper in
their burning ears, "I am what you fear most. I am
your nightmare come to life. I am a performance artist.
And you are part of my act. I know your name and I'm
not afraid to use it. What you say to me definitely
does not go in one ear and out the other. No matter
what you have fooled yourself into thinking. What you
say stays right between my ears and comes out of my
mouth in downtown performance spaces where I tell the
captive audience of how you used your attraction for
me to humiliate me. And everyone's on my side." Like I
said, just another day. Just another temp job.

Had brunch with my parents and my sister and her fiancé today. My sister's wedding is impending and everyone's just AFLUTTER. My parents were bugging me (as usual) and I thought: Life is just one huge mental de-infestation. You bomb, you spray, you put out traps for the scrambling remnants of ancestral influence that continue to live inside your mind. You play host to masses of opinionated parental pupae ready to hatch at any moment. Assert your independence, trust yourself, ignore their advice and the hordes appear, ready to judge, manipulate, and subvert. They feed off of your fear and insecurity. Vulnerability is their Cracker Jack. And just when you think you have the problem under control...you're tired one night and you go to bed without washing the emotional dishes. When you wake up, signs of your parents are everywhere, in everything, swarming, infecting, fighting amongst themselves in your head. There is no relief. They're immune to every poison. There's no off-the-shelf product that can get rid of this kind of persistent vermin. They'll just live on in you until there's nothing left for them to feed on. Then they'll migrate to another unsuspecting host who lazily left a box of her feelings open on the counter of her psyche.

My Eggs Benedict was good.

If you're over thirty,
you don't *have* to take your parents' advice.

You can. Of course. If you want to.
And if taking it doesn't make you feel like you're still a child.
And if somehow you are able to convince yourself
that their advice is solid and grounded
and takes into account how well they know you
and how right they've been in the past.
If you can take their advice under those conditions,
well, lucky you.

compromise

{ Lowering my standards.

So you can meet them. }

ADVICE FROM **ANITA LIBERTY**

The Best Way to Eat Kiwi Fruit

Without skinning the fruit,
slice the kiwi in half (width-wise).
Eat the inside out using a spoon.

Mmm.

Delicious.

Got a letter from Bart, an old college friend.
I had heard that he had come through New York on a
business trip and hadn't called me. So I wrote to him
to find out what was up with that. We'd been out of
touch for a while, but I always expected that we'd
call each other whenever we were in each other's
vicinity. Bart was one of my best friends at school.
Well, sure we slept together, but that's what you
did in college. That doesn't mean that we were ever
romantically involved. Anyway, here's his letter in
its entirety:

Dear Anita:

I got your letter today. Yes, I was in New York
this week and no, I did not call you. To be honest, I did not (and do not) feel comfortable seeing women who I have spent time with in the
past, given that I am currently (and forever)
involved with my fiancée, Wendy. Frankly, I am
surprised that this is not apparent to you. Maybe
we're different, but it just doesn't sit well with
me. This means that, in some cases, I do not see
or correspond with old friends. I'm sorry if this
upsets you, but that's simply the way that it is
for me.

Sincerely,

Bart

Hmm. I have to sleep on this one.

　　The next morning: Got it. Bart has neglected to
consider that just as it takes two people to begin a
friendship, it takes two to end it. I've still got his
number. And I plan to use it. I'll leave messages on
his machine. Cute messages. Intimate, cooing, nostalgic
whispers. At some point during the message, I'll gig-
gle. I know where he lives. So I'll write to him, too.
He'll get missives full of memories and private jokes

and things that only a jealous woman would understand. I know his fiancée, Wendy, will read them, because I'll make it easy for her. I'll send postcards. I'll never once refer to her or to their engagement. I'll treat him as if he were still single. "But doesn't she even know about me?" his precious Wendy will whine. And he will spend all of his time making excuses. Digging out the seeds I have planted before they take root in her mind. Scrambling to prove himself innocent for a crime he didn't commit. Big fights with his fiancée. That's what he gets for writing me off. Someone acts like a stupid jerk, I get even. I'm sorry if this upsets him, but that's simply the way that it is for me.

Your
absence
has
not
made
my
heart

grow
fonder.

Running Into You

You.
You.
You.
You would be who?
Do I know you?
Did we go to the same
high school,
college,
camp,
kindergarten?
Did you date my sister?
Do you live in my neighborhood?
Do we take the same subway?
Have I seen you at the gym?
   No, clearly that's not it.
Come on.
Give me a hint.
I'm racking my brain,
waiting for the bell to start ringing,
trying to place the face.

You.
You.
You.
You would be who?
Do I know you?
Oh my God. It's you.
You.
The sociopath
Who I went out with for three and a half years?
Who I lived with for four months?
Who left me for a woman named Heather?
Mitchell? Is that you?

Huh.
Funny I didn't remember you.
I see now that you haven't changed a bit.
I'm so, so sorry.
That must be terrible.
To still be you.

ADVICE FROM **ANITA LIBERTY**

If you run into someone who's broken your heart,
act like you don't know him.
Act like you've drawn a blank.
Act like you've never seen him before,
even if you really want to whack his fucking black baseball cap
off his ugly head and kick his ass when he bends down to pick it up.

I thought you were a tortured and gifted artist.

I was wrong. About the gifted part.
Oh. And the artist part.

It's one thing to count on retaining your composure
if *you* run into your ex on the street,
it's another to count on your friends being able to think on their feet.
You can't.
That's why you should compose a letter
to each of your close friends outlining
the approved procedure for an unplanned interaction
(which should be the only kind they have,
if they're *really* your friends).

Here's mine: ⟶

Dear Friend of Anita's,

Should you have the unfortunate experience of
encountering my ex-boyfriend, Mitchell, on the street,
at the movies, at a party (wait, if you're there and he's
there, where am I and why wasn't I invited?), you may
be confused about the appropriate way to greet him.
Let me tell you to ease the burden of your having to
come up with something on your own.

First of all, the whole time you're talking to
him, you have to remember, vividly and emotionally,
what he put me through. You have to remember that I
called you 14 times a day, in the middle of the night,
first thing in the morning, at work and at home. That
will help. You have to look at him and know, better
than your own name, that he hurt someone you love.
Don't touch him. Keep your hands to yourself. Physical
violence doesn't solve anything. And, besides, he'll
just run away.

With all of this in mind, get the speech ready.
The one I'm helping you to prepare. Say that you've
actually been thinking about him recently, wondering
how he could have made such a stupid mistake as letting me go, just when my career is taking off, and I'm
in such demand, personally and professionally. Say
that you really feel sorry for him, that it's one thing
to go through a break-up and try to move on, but another to leave someone and have to realize every day that
you've made some kind of irreparable, brutal error in
judgment. God. That must be awful. Is he okay with
that? Okay with the fact that his ex-girlfriend is
basing her entire, flourishing career on publicly
humiliating him? And that I have a following? And
that everyone, even strangers, know what an asshole
he is and how badly he dumped me? Me. Your most suc-
cessful and talented friend?

Does he wake up in the middle of the night
thinking that he sacrificed the one person that gave
his life any worth at all? The one person who goes out
on dates EVERY WEEKEND (and sometimes during the week
when her weekends get too full). The one person who
has to turn down invitations to fabulous parties,
because she's already committed to making an appear-
ance at other fabulous parties? That one person who
loved him despite his many noticeable flaws? The one

person who can barely return phone calls, because her time is so full with productivity and the rewards that come with finding one's true calling and getting paid obscene amounts of money to keep doing the very thing that comes as easy to her as breathing? The one person who, although she continues to write many exuberant and moving poems about her ex-boyfriend, has personally moved right the hell along in her life without looking back at the man who wasted all of her time? The one person who doesn't even think about him anymore? That one?

Then before he has a chance to tell you anything about himself and what he's doing or what he considers to be his accomplishments, say you gotta go and leave. Just walk away. Fast. Leave him dazed and regretful. More than he normally is.

Thanks for being a good friend.

Sincerely,

Anita Liberty

Obviously, you should tailor this letter to your own personal needs and circumstances.
Details close to the truth are the most effective device.
Make your friends sign something that binds them to serving in your best interest.
Make them remember that it's not just you who suffered,
they suffered, too.
You may not have to remind them,
they may remember on their own and act accordingly when Mitchell or,
rather, *your* ex stumbles unwittingly across their paths.

EXCERPT FROM **ANITA LIBERTY'S DIARY**

When I ran into him, Mitchell told me not to dwell on things that happened in the past, that there's no point in getting mad about something all over again. He's so oily. Well, I have to dwell on something...it might as well be all those times he hurt me. Who said time heals all? I say time heals nothing. Because each new injustice takes its cue from the one before, and the one before that, and the one before that, and the one before that, and the one before that, and the one before that, and the one before that, and the one before that, BECAUSE THAT WAS THE WORST ONE.

He doesn't realize it, but I'm doing him a favor, really. If I don't hold him accountable for his actions, who will?

I know what people say about me.

"Anita Liberty's **so angry.**"
"Anita Liberty's so **angry at men.**"
"Anita Liberty just **needs to get laid.**"

And I'm like, you know…

duh!

Guys Who Want to Sleep with Me
and the Things They Say That Make Me Say No

You seem like you're a very strong woman.
I just broke up with someone two weeks ago who I went
out with for two years and I'm totally over it.
Do a poem for me right now.
Are you always this angry?
Do you hate all men?
Your show is a hoot.
Do you get naked on stage?
What's your real job?
What's your real name?
I do stand-up.
I'm a feminist in my own way.
Do you want to get fresh?
Are you going to write a poem about me?
So you're an actress?
I love the films of Ed Burns.
I was born in 1972.
I cut my own hair.
We'll laugh about this at our wedding.

No Bad Dates

Never call a first date a *date*.That way, if it doesn't work out,
you haven't had a bad *date*, you've just met someone
with whom you don't intend to waste any more of your time.
If it does work out, then you can call it a *date* after the fact.
Fail-safe.

Blind Date

Never again.
Ever.
I mean it.
Never will I trust
anyone's judgment but my own.
But it's just one night, they say.
What's one night?
One night.
Don't ever tell me how to waste my time.
A friend of the family
knows a single young man.
On the basis of that information
and on that information alone,
my father gave them my number.
Now someone I don't know has my number —
already a bumbling misstep over my personal boundaries.
    He calls.
    I hate his voice.
    We meet.
    We eat.
I wear a see-through shirt with nothing underneath,
just to taunt him.
Just so the evening's not a total waste.
    I talk poetry.
    He talks investment banking.
    I talk life.
    He talks business.
What a brilliant match this was.
Whose idea was this anyway?
So well thought-out and considerate.
We have so much in common.
Like we both have skin.
That's certainly enough to base a
relationship on.
Then I notice his hands as he
nibbles demurely on his eggroll.
They are tiny.
Minute, even.
Barely able to find their way out of the sleeves
of his navy blue blazer,
they clutch at the morsel of food between them.

The aroma of my ginger chicken is quickly overpowered
by the pungent smell of cedar chips.
And as I stare,
his nails turn to claws
and I have lost sight of his opposable thumbs.
Fine blond fur coats his... **paws.**

I know now (for sure) that I can have
no future with this man.
Even if we were able to overcome
our differences,
and start a family,
I'd always be nervous
that when my back was turned,
he would devour our young.

My Friend's Boyfriend's Friend Thinks I'm Cute

So this guy wants to go on a date with me.
And yes, I've met him.
And no, I'm not attracted to him.
But I'm trying to be open.

He wants to meet at my apartment.
   Okay.
He wants to talk before we go out to dinner.
   Okay.
He wants to talk about the woman he just broke up with.
   Okay.
He sounds like a dick and I'm totally on her side and,
in fact, am wishing I were having her evening right now.
No matter what she's doing, she's doing it without him.

We go to dinner.
While we're waiting for the maitre d' to get our table ready,
I feel something unfamiliar on the back of my neck.
It's a hand.
It's his hand.
His hand is on the back of my neck.
Get it off. **Get it off.**
Oh God.
Quick, somebody, just get it off.
Our table is ready.
The hand is removed.

After dinner
(he ordered skate, I ordered soup,
we split the bill 50-50, which means
that I totally just paid for some of his skate)
we go back to my apartment.
His idea.
(I'm trying to be open, remember?)
I stand by the door
and he sits on my couch.
He wants to talk.
Again?
I mean, okay.

I sit down on a chair to hear him talk.
The next thing I know, he's no longer
on the couch. Where is he?
I've lost track of the little rascal.
And then I feel it again.
It's the hand.
And it's on the back of my neck again.

Get it off, I scream.

And he is gone.
His hand, the money he saved on his skate and all.

I know now (for sure) that I can have
no future with this man.
**Because I can't stand
the feel of his fucking hand
on my neck.**

Sex-Guy

He takes off his shirt
and I see he's wearing something underneath.
It's some sort of...costume.
There's a huge **S** emblazoned across his chest.
Is it...
Could it be...
I think it looks like...
It is.
It's "Sex-Guy."

You know him.
You've probably even slept with him.
Sex-Guy gives women what they want.
Or what he thinks they want.
He's a sexual superhero.
Or so he thinks.

And his mission begins.
His voice has gotten lower.
He's talking dirty.
He's making me want it.
Bad.
Really bad.

"Is this what you want?
You want this, don't you?
How much do you want it?"
    "Yes, that is what I want.
    Yes, I want that.
    I want it. Bad. Really bad."

(Funny how when I'm masturbating
I fantasize that I'm not alone,
and now that I'm not alone,
I'm fantasizing about masturbating.)

He works fast.
He works hard.
His work is done.
Or that's what he thinks.
He's "Sex-Guy" and he saved another woman

from abstinence.
Rescued her from the dreariness of another night
of self-love.
He's "Sex-Guy."
And if anyone can give a woman eight orgasms in
twenty minutes, he can.

But he didn't.

ADVICE FROM **ANITA LIBERTY**

I try not to gear the advice I give to one specific gender, or, you know, the other, but I thought that everyone might benefit if I were as direct and pointed as possible.

TO MEN: If a woman agrees to have sex with you, chances are she likes you and you should try to be nice to someone who likes you. Or at least polite. If she agrees to have sex with you more than once, like maybe many times over the course of a couple of weeks, she really, really likes you and her feelings may get hurt when she reasonably expects that you will treat her as if you like her, too. After all, you liked her enough to have sex with her, you should like her enough to return her calls or give her an explanation as to why you won't. She deserves that. Pretty much everyone deserves that, but especially everyone you've seen naked.

TO WOMEN: Don't have sex with him until you're sure you can trust him. That is, unless you're just having sex to fulfill a primal desire and you haven't been touched in months and you don't have strong feelings either way and there's no possible way that he could hurt whatever feelings you might have.
If that's your reason, go for it.

Monkey See

I went on a date with a man
who was so obsessed with primates
that everything in his apartment
was in the shape of a chimpanzee.
Lamps, statuettes, magnets, mugs, stuffed animals.
And, on his bed, sheets with monkeys on them.
He was 35.
Sheets with monkeys on them.
35.
Monkey sheets.

Another Blind Date

I pick him up at his apartment.
Based solely on his looks,
I'm not physically unattracted to him.
He has a certain magnetism.
A blondness.

He runs the family business.
Pipes. Fittings. Drains.
Did I say pipes?
I don't know.
Something useful is manufactured under his direction.

It's dinnertime.
Sushi. Saki. Another saki.
We start talking about dating.
Previous relationships.
And such.
He says that the last woman he dated
is getting married and he doesn't think
she's making the right decision.
She's not marrying the right guy.
I'm like, well, you can't tell her who to marry
if she wants to get married and
you're not willing to marry her.
And he's like, oh, I told her I'd marry her.
When?
Last week.
When's she getting married?
Next week.
Oh my.
Did she say no?
(Like I should have when he asked me to dinner?)
She hasn't told him either way yet.
She has a week.

I spent the evening with a republican
(did I mention that?)
who has an outstanding marriage proposal.

I said that based on his looks,
I wasn't physically unattracted to him.
This is true.
But based on his personality,
I'm intellectually revolted.

Date with the Devil

How often do you get the chance?
He spotted me.
Across a crowded room.
Zeroed in.
Threw in the line.
I took the bait.
He told me that he was going to be an astronaut
but changed his mind and became a novelist.
(Swoon.)
He threw money around.
I was wined and dined.
He "confessed" that he hadn't felt this close
to anyone
in such a long time.
I believed him.
Why wouldn't I?
He's convincing.
He's trained to seduce.
It's his job.
I did my research.
Asked around.
Found out only terrible things about him.
A truly tarnished reputation.
Born bad.
Someone called him "The Devil."
So I slept with him.
I mean, who wouldn't sleep with the devil?
He's got to be pretty good in bed with that
    kind of notability.
He wasn't.
He wasn't the Devil,
just one of his harmless, ineffective, little, tiny,
    insignificant, small (really small) helpers.

Don't trust anyone
who, after knowing you for all of four hours, tells you
that they've never felt so connected to, so moved by,
so comfortable with, someone as he/she feels with you.

It's just not true.
Well, he/she may think it's true. And you are pretty great,
but he/she's just looking for something that he/she
will find out you can't deliver and then he/she will
discover that you're just a normal person.
A really sexy, cool, well-adjusted normal person,
but a normal person all the same.

And he/she will realize this and stop calling.
Just stop calling. And his/her desperation to see you again
and desire to spend every minute with you will fade away
and be replaced with a palpable ambivalence. And then
you're the one who ends up getting disappointed.

Avoid that.

I don't hate men. I think that's a common misconception about me that I really want to clarify. I don't hate men. Not all men. One man hurt me really badly and, yes, I do hate him. Mitchell. And I do go on dates that don't work out. I don't hate those men. I don't care enough about those men to hate them. I just like to make fun of them. And I don't dismiss all men, just because I happened to encounter one bad man. If I hated all men, I wouldn't date them. And then I'd have nothing to write about and I'd be bored. (And so would you.)

Smarter than You
or
Yet Another Blind Date
or
When Will I Learn?
or
I'm Not *that* Desperate
or
Maybe I Am

You sit in judgment of me
while I speak words you don't understand.
Admit it.
This is going right over your — head.
Don't pretend to look interested,
captivated...
let the ignorance wash over you
like a protective blanket,
and then we'll both be happy,
or at least whatever the opposite
of desperate is.
Excuse me if I know everything about everything,
but I do.
And this modern-day Eve won't be ashamed.
Don't worry, I'll sleep with you whether or not you
discern my art.
If I used people's acceptance as a measure for
intimate inclusion in my life,
I'd be a lonely woman.
As a matter of fact,

I am.

I'm a Pond

He called me a pond.
I was being sensitive
(like I know how to be anything else)
and he said that I was like a little pond.

I thought, fuck you.
I am not a pond.
A little, still, little pond.
As if anyone could walk by and kick something in me
disrupting my placidity.
Muddy and filled with weeds.
Pebbles disturbing me.
People trampling on me,
splashing around,
kicking through,
and leaving.
I am not a pond.
A sensitive, little, easily defeated pond.

And then I thought,
wait. A pond's pretty big.
I'm thinking of a puddle.
I'm not a puddle.
I'm okay with being a pond,
but I'm no puddle.

anchorotize

{
Staying celibate so that you can conserve
and redirect your sexual energy.
A good word to know if you're just not getting any.
"I'm not a loser, I'm anchorotizing."
}

I'm uptight. Wound once too many times. Type
Triple A. That's me. There's got to be a solution.
Shopping. No, not for clothes. Too much the kind of
cliché I spend all my time trying to avoid. I'm looking
for something that will help me see the light and get
out of the tunnel of despair in which I seem to have
gotten lost. So I went to a candle store and realized
that I can have everything I ever wanted for just
$9.95. I will have no more anxiety when I light the
candle with the "Relaxation" label slapped on its side.
I won't be depressed if the wick on my "Happiness Is
Yours" candle burns bright. There won't be any need to
actually ponder my life because "Meditation" will do it
for me. And I won't have to actually date anyone if I
remember to ignite the "Attraction/Love" taper as soon
as I get home. Why get a job when "Prosperity" will
come as soon as I flick my "Bic?" And my therapist will
be out one patient when I kindle the candle labeled
"You Are Not Your Parents." I bought them all. But the
one candle I can't seem to find (the one that doesn't
smell of bergamot, lavender, patchouli, ylang-ylang,
jasmine, or sandalwood, but instead reeks of resent-
ment and has the stench of truth) is the one with the
label that reads: "Your Ex-Boyfriend's Not Worth Your
Time And You're So Much Better Off Without Him And
Who Cares If He Does Have A New Girlfriend, That
Doesn't Mean He's Happy." That's the one candle that
I will keep lit eternally like the Olympic flame.
The only one that will truly allow me light in the
darkness. The only one truly worth every one of those
995 pennies.

Attracting My Opposite

I am an unfriendly person.
I really am.
I am judgmental.
I am critical.
I am unforgiving.
I don't like small talk.

So how did we find each other?
Is this some sort of cruel joke?

I wanted a dog.
A dog to keep me company.
To keep me company so I wouldn't have to interact
with people who don't deserve me.
I wanted a dog as unfriendly as I am.

I didn't get that.
I got Daphne.
And Daphne is friendly.
Very fucking friendly.
Daphne may be the friendliest
fucking dog on the planet.

She demands the attention of
every single person that I avoid.
Licks, wiggles, and nuzzles
the calves of people who
would never command my time.

She has a different set of standards...
as in she has none.
I've tried to teach her to be cold,
unfeeling,
aloof.

She just doesn't get it.
She lives for some stranger's touch.
The taste of a stranger's hand.
Anyone is safe.
She trusts everyone.
Stupid dog.
Stupid Daphne. Stupid, cute, friendly, fucking
hypoallergenic nightmare.

EXCERPT FROM **ANITA LIBERTY'S DIARY**

I was on this same temp job for weeks. I felt
like a full-time employee. I knew that one day it
would end, but I always thought I'd be the one to
leave. That's why I was surprised when the office man-
ager called me into her office, shut the door, and
fired me. Can you be fired from a temp job? I didn't
think so. And I have to say that I'm confused because
I was so fond of the paycheck every week. I liked the
free long distance. And the Power Macs. I really
enjoyed the way that I could get away with going in
there and doing my own work. It's not my fault they
caught on. Why should I be the one who gets punished?
Well, I don't want to go. They can't make me...go back
to having to buy my own office supplies. I don't want
casual Fridays to be every day of my week. I don't even
know how much it costs to call California. I could get
really screwed on my phone bill next month. I decided
not to beg. They're not worth it. I'm just going to go
find some other company's time and money to waste.
Reproduce my art on some other company's Xerox copier.
Take advantage of some other company's advantages.
Then we'll see how they feel. That'll serve them right.
To have to watch me use someone else the way that I
used them.

Liberty Rules

You cannot know how I am.
You cannot call me.
You cannot even know my number.
You cannot know where I live.
You cannot be in my neighborhood.
In fact, you can't be in any neighborhood but your own.

When we broke up, you got the East Village.
I got everywhere else.
Don't complain.
First Avenue to Third.
Fourteenth Street to St. Mark's.
That's yours.
There are delis.
You won't starve.
There are clothing stores.
You won't freeze.
There's a movie theater.
Two, in fact.
And bookstores.
And a tattoo parlor if you want to get a tattoo.
If you're interested, I have some ideas
of what should be tattooed on you
and where.
You cannot leave the East Village unless you have to go to
a doctor in another neighborhood and even then the illness
has to be life-threatening.
You cannot perform where I perform.
You cannot show up where I'm going to be.
And, if you do, you have to leave.
You cannot know where I live.
You cannot call me.
You cannot even know my number.
You cannot call my friends.
You cannot ask my friend's husband to take
your headshots.
You cannot send my parents a Christmas card.
Who the fuck do you think you are?
Martha Stewart?
Well, listen, Martha, those are the rules.
Follow them and no one will get hurt. Again.

So be happy and stay where you are.
Stay.
Stay.
I said, stay.

I don't want to stay where I am.
And, unlike Mitchell, I don't have to.

I can't believe it. It's too good to be true. I
woke up this morning not thinking about Mitchell!!!!!!

Spent the day not thinking about Mitchell!

EXCERPT FROM **ANITA LIBERTY'S DIARY**

Still not thinking about Mitchell!

they
can smell it
when
you're
moving on

I used to have **dreams** that Mitchell came back to me.
I still do. nightmares.
But now I call them

Guys Who I Want to Sleep with and the Things I Say That Make Them Say "Yes. Oh God...YES!"

Hi. How are you?

Those Things

I'm tormented.
I can't stop thinking about all those awful things I said to you.
I want to take it all back.
I want to turn back the clock.

You didn't deserve to hear those things.
I should have been more careful.
I should have been more thoughtful.
I didn't mean it. Any of it.

Like the time I said you were incredibly attractive.
Not true.
Or the time I said you could do anything you set your mind to.
You can't.
Or the time I said you were the only person
who could make me laugh.
Don't make me laugh.
Or the time I said you had plenty of hair left.
Don't make me laugh.

I look back and realize that I was blind.
But now that my eyes have been forced open
by your departure,
I'm relieved to finally tell the truth:
My parents never liked you.
Your writing is awkward and uncomfortably self-conscious.
You shouldn't be allowed to drive.
And you look really bad naked.

perspicuous

{ I am. }

EXCERPT FROM **ANITA LIBERTY'S DIARY**

No temp job. So I stayed home and organized my
own life, instead of someone else's. I sorted, I consoli-
dated, I filed. I filed the boys. Chronologically in
the box under my bed. The box that stores the boys. The
boy-box. They all live there now: The first boy I slept
with, the one I moved in with, the older man, the
younger man, the musician, the playwright. And now
Mitchell. The best things he ever wrote. The campaign
promises. The tomes of love and affection and FOREVER
written every time until the end. I'm closing the box
now. I'm sure you boys have a lot to talk about. You
certainly have a lot in common. You're all depressed,
self-destructive, and in emotional denial. All lucky
to have met me and all stupid to have let me go.

Went to the Poetry Club tonight. When I got there, the owner handed me a letter that had come addressed to me in care of the club. Here's what it said:

Dear Anita:

I have a crush on you. I've seen you at the Poetry Club and I really think I'm in love. Last week you confessed to the audience that you sometimes bite your nails. I do, too! How exciting! We have so much in common. I can tell we'd get along wonderfully. If only, alas, you would notice me. I'm much too shy to approach you in person. If only I could think of one thing -- one little hook -- that would provoke a favorable response. A person -- nay, a beautiful person -- of your wit and charm must get hundreds of letters each day. How to be the one, the one noticed and preferred above all others? A hopeless task. Yet I must attempt. I must endure. I must type like I've never typed before. Aye, mateys...prepare the spell-checks! Batten down the compliments! Hoist the sail of truth and flattery, and ride the winds of chance! Keep yer eyes on yonder horizon, mates, for the first to spot land shall win the prize -- a kiss from the beautiful Lady Liberty. Maybe.

Love,
An Admirer

My first fan letter. I have no idea who sent that to me, but I'd do him.

ADVICE FROM **ANITA LIBERTY**

Buy eye gel.
Put it in the refrigerator.
Then when you put it on,
you'll feel fresh.

What? I'm beautiful.
I can give beauty tips.
It's allowed.
My book, my advice.

liberty

{
To have the run of;
to have one's own way;
to have one's fling;
to stand on one's own feet;
to stand on one's rights;
to have a will of one's own;
to paddle one's own canoe;
to play a lone hand.
}

Is it possible to plagiarize a thesaurus?

Went to a party tonight. A party made up of two
categories: stars and starfuckers. It was as delineat-
ed as gender. But what about me? Where did I fit in? I
want to be a star, not fuck one. This guy approached me
and within, I'd say, forty-five seconds had dropped
about twelve names. First names. Names I was supposed
to recognize. Names by which I was supposed to be
impressed. Apparently, he's a close personal friend of
Ethan's. According to him, Ethan's phone number is in
his book, but he never has to look it up because...HE
HAS ETHAN'S NUMBER MEMORIZED! Really, he's not like
those other people who just **say** they're friends with
Ethan, he really **is** a friend of Ethan's. Ethan doesn't
waste his time with just anyone, he assures me, Ethan
wastes his time with him. Ethan sets him up on dates
with otherwise unattainable women. But because he's a
friend of Ethan's, women want him. (Other women want
him.) Ethan asks him for advice and invites him to
parties and lets him casually drop his name in conver-
sations with strangers who might be impressed that he
knows, no, has hung out with, no, is **actually FRIENDS
WITH ETHAN**. The weird thing about this encounter was
that it wasn't the first time Ethan's name has come up
as a tool of seduction. Ethan has a lot of close, personal friends and I think I've met all of them. And I
wonder, if I'm meeting all of Ethan's friends, is Ethan
meeting all of mine? Ethan should know that someday
he is going to run into a **FRIEND OF ANITA's** and he
should be scared.

HOST

Welcome to an evening of the best of our open mike nights. I've invited some of our most interesting and beloved performers to present some of their newer, and riskier, material to you, the brave and willing audience. To open tonight's festivities, I bring you a fairly new presence to The Poetry Club stage, but one who I hope, and desire, becomes a regular to our humble dais. Please welcome, gentlemen and gentlewomen, Anita Liberty.

[*Applause.*]

ANITA LIBERTY

Good evening. I am Anita Liberty. I'll keep this short and sweet. I call this poem, "Charting My Progress."

Things can't be all bad.
I know a starfucker
who wants to fuck me.

[*Silence. Then...applause.*]

ANITA LIBERTY (cont'd.)

Thank you.

[*Aggressively enthusiastic applause from the sophisticated and discerning audience continues for a ridiculously long time. It doesn't stop. Not until long after Anita Liberty has left the building.*]

EXCERPT FROM **ANITA LIBERTY'S DIARY**

I was moving on. MOVING ON. Finally. And like
nerve gas through a crack in the door, Mitchell infil-
trated the walls of my emotional fortress through the
mail. I got a letter from him today. Samantha was with
me when I got it. She thought I should make copies and
plaster them around his neighborhood. It was a card
with a picture of a forlorn gorilla on the front. A
sad, dejected, sorry-looking primate. Gee, I wonder
why he picked **that** card. He wants me back. That was
the gist. So now what? What?

They can smell it when you're moving on.
They can. And he did.
So now what? Ignore him?
No, that would be too polite.
And you may miss him.

And you may be able to forget that
he treated you with total and
decided disrespect. Maybe.

But however you feel and whatever you decide to do,
you can count on the fact that he hasn't changed
and he probably never will.
That's okay, as long as you use this moment of his
self-professed vulnerability and regret to get exactly what you want.
If he really wants you back, really *wants* you, he'll make some promises.
And you need to protect yourself the way you would before entering
into any agreement.

GET IT IN WRITING.
Before you say yes.
Before you tell your friends the good (?) news.
Before you sleep with him.
Create a paper trail. Keep all documentation.
If he calls you, keep the answering machine messages.
If he writes letters, laminate them.
Demand sufficient, tangible evidence.
Then if he ever does go back on his word,
you can shove his word in his face.

If you want anything at all, ask for it now.
He's put you through a lot.
You shouldn't take him back, but if you do,
get something else as well.

You can be bought. For the right price.

This can be a great time in a relationship.
You didn't want to break up.
You wished and wished for him to return.
You begged. He ignored you. You got over him.

And now, and only now, is he back.
It's his turn to beg.
Let him beg, if he wants to beg.
Let him beg for a long time.

Hear his apologies and weigh your options.
It's like a job offer.
Once he puts out his initial offer, you can either accept it, reject it,
or hold out for a better deal.

Here's a hint:
Hold out.

Wake-Up Call

To sink into you
and sleep for a long time.
To lie against you,
breathing,
sleeping,
lost,
free,
where I wanted to be.
Nowhere.
With you.

But you woke up first
and left while my eyes were still closed,
And I woke up alone.

Now I'm wide awake.
And I realize that there's more to see
when I have my eyes open.

I'm wide awake.
The sun's up and it's in my eyes.
I won't close them again
without seeing.
And you want me to sleep with you again.
I realize that that's all I was doing with you.
Sleeping.
I'm not tired anymore.
Not anymore.
I'm on a caffeine high
that might just last for the rest of my life.

bliss

{ When someone dumps you
and you get over it and you're not thinking about him
(at all) and then he comes back to you and
begs for your forgiveness and you haven't decided
to give it to him yet. }

I decided to write back to Mitchell. Here's what I wrote:

Dear Mitchell,

I got your card in the mail yesterday. I was surprised at how vulnerable you seemed. How unguarded. Exposed even. I was so surprised in fact that I showed your card to everyone.

My best friend was with me when I got it, so I had to show it to her. She thinks I'm lucky. None of her ex-boyfriends have ever come crawling back.

I was going to have dinner with my sister that night and since I had the card with me, I showed it to her too. She said that when you apologize for not having been a more attentive lover, you actually seem pretty sincere.

I guess my sister must have told my parents that I had gotten a card from you, so of course they wanted to see it. After reading it, my mom said she felt sorry for you and why didn't I give you a second chance. My dad said that you were right, I did deserve better and a friend of the family knows another single young man who wants to meet me.

My next door neighbor marked it as the sign of a desperate man, but the doorman was able to discern a certain strength of conviction, especially when you said that you'd never be able to find someone as smart and beautiful as I am.

I read it aloud to a packed house at the Poetry Club. Everyone laughed.

I faxed a copy to the New York Times on a whim
and now Anna Quindlen wants to return to the
Times to do a guest column, print the card in
its entirety, and title it "Men and the Cult of
Delayed Self-Awareness."

I looked at the card again by myself before I
went to bed. There's really nothing between the
lines. It's all there in black and white. You
miss me. You want me back. I won. I knew I would.
But now I have it in writing.

Not yours yet,
Anita

I'm confused. I enjoy my space, but I get lonely
sometimes. I want to be independent, but I need to be
taken care of. I'm not looking for another relationship, but I'm scared I'll never find one. Maybe I miss
Mitchell. Maybe I just miss being in a relationship.
He says he's changed. But the truth is that I changed
him. I changed him into this incredibly great guy
and then he dumped me because he thought he deserved
better than me. Who's to say that that wouldn't happen
again? Anyway, the timing couldn't be better. My
younger sister's getting married tomorrow. A while
ago, she asked me to write a poem to read at her
wedding. "What kind of poem?" I asked her. "A nice
poem," she replied. I haven't even put pen to paper
and the wedding's in twelve hours.

A Nice Poem
The poem I read at my sister's wedding

Who has the veil?
Hide the bride.
Where's the groom?
Hide the bride.
Is it almost time?
Hide the bride.
And hide the bride we will.
We shall cover her frequently showered
body with layers of chiffon, satin, tulle, silk
(raw and refined).
My younger sister's getting married.
She's getting married.
Here she comes.
She's walking down the aisle.
Here she comes.
She's getting closer.
Here she comes.
Quick, hide the bride.
Drink white champagne in white crystal.
Eat white cake with white frosting.
Hold white flowers with white ribbon.
As the white girl in the white dress
meets the black-haired man in the
black tuxedo waiting at the end of
the aisle to unveil what we have
so cleverly disguised.
Hide...

....the

bride!

A Wasted Life
The poem I wanted to read at my sister's wedding

I threw you your goddamned shower
and made everyone dress up
like a different time of day and night
just like you wanted.
I will endure the questions, the stares, the pity
when everyone asks me why
I haven't found someone yet
and does it bother me that my younger sister
is getting married before I am.
Why aren't you getting married?
They'll ask me.
Why aren't you getting married?
Why aren't you getting married?
Maybe because I'm not ready.
Maybe because I don't want to.
Maybe because I haven't found the right person yet.
Maybe because I don't even have a goddamned boyfriend.
Nobody will care that I am a well-established and
well-respected poet.
No, they won't be interested in my mind.
It's my younger sister's wedding and the only part of
anyone's body that will get noticed
is the third finger of the left hand.
(I'm thinking of tattooing mine with the words "Fuck off.")
And blissfully unaware of my gnawing contempt,
my sister, by blood and blood alone,
will walk down the aisle.
The aisle.
The aisle paved with the souls
of women locked in a silent scream
of regret and wasted dreams.
The women whose satin-heeled feet
clip-clopped towards a future
of cloying and insincere promise.
Women, who willfully promenade
from one man to the next.
Given, as it were and as it will always be, away
by a man who never held the deed of ownership
to another who never will.

While I spend just about all of my time
deconstructing and devaluing the
fragile legend of the woman's role in this world,
my sister, born of the same womb as I,
will walk numbly down the aisle,
and leave yet another gutted shell underneath
the dainty step of society's next victim
of tradition.

For Mitchell Love Liberty (#3 in the Trilogy)

I wish we were back together
if only for one night
so I could watch you as you fell asleep,
then tie you gently down,
and tattoo you.

Right over where your heart should be,
it will be scripted in India ink:
Abandon all hope ye
who enter here.
For more information,
call Anita Liberty
at 212–978–7955.

Hey, nothing's permanent.
(You taught me that.)
I'm sure you'll be able to get it removed.
For a lot of money, a lot of time,
and
a lot
of
pain.
And it may leave a scar.

But before it goes,
maybe someone will see it
and she will have been saved.
And I will have saved her.
Saved her a lot of money,
a lot of time,
and
a lot
of
pain.
And she will not be scarred for life.

If I save just one woman from you,
I will consider my mission accomplished
and I will have found peace.

You hurt me,
I tattoo you.
It's only fair.

Don't take him back.

independence day

Independence Day

Alone, alone, alone.
Awake alone.
Asleep alone.
Weeks alone.
Weekends alone.
Home alone.
Not home alone.
Just alone.
But alone by choice.
Mustn't ever forget that.
I don't have to be alone.
I want to be alone.
I made the choice.
I'm an independent woman.
I am strong.
In fact, every day is Independence Day for Anita Liberty.
Free from another's opinions.
Free from your judgment.
Free from the shackles of a decidedly patriarchal morality.
Free from the chains of having to please —
a man.
I am strong.
I am single.
I am alone.
Alone, alone, alone.
I don't need anybody,
especially you.

all's well that ends

[*EXCERPT FROM TRANSCRIPT OF "ANITA LIBERTY LIVE —
ONE NIGHT ONLY — BACK BY POPULAR DEMAND — IN A
BENEFIT TO SAVE THE POETRY CLUB," NEW YORK CITY,
RECORDED LIVE ON DECEMBER 1, 1998*]

MAYA ANGELOU

And now I have the pleasure of introducing my
close, personal friend. I am in awe of her talent,
her composure, her drive. I learn from her. And
she is a willing and gracious teacher. Ladies and
gentlemen, Anita Liberty.

[*Deafening applause as the audience rises to its
feet and welcomes Anita Liberty to the stage.*]

ANITA LIBERTY

Thank you.

[*Applause doesn't show any signs of slowing down.*]

ANITA LIBERTY (cont'd.)

Thank you. I...

[*The crowd, still on its feet, continues its ova-
tion.*]

ANITA LIBERTY (cont'd.)

Please. I acknowledge and appreciate your adora-
tion. Now sit and be quiet so I can talk about
myself.

[*Audience sits and is quiet.*]

ANITA LIBERTY (cont'd.)

Good evening. As you all know, I am Anita Liberty.
As you also all know, my boyfriend, Mitchell —

[*Audience boos in unison.*]

ANITA LIBERTY (cont'd.)

— my boyfriend, Mitchell, left me for a woman named
Heather and, to get even, I devoted my entire
career to humiliating him in public. I have publicly humiliated Mitchell in every medium: television, film, magazines, newspapers, the Internet,

and, of course, my best-selling book *How to Heal
the Hurt by Hating.*

[*Audience cheers.*]

                    ANITA LIBERTY (cont'd.)
Ten weeks on the "List."

[*More applause.*]

                    ANITA LIBERTY (cont'd.)
Now, I'd like to be able to get up here tonight and
say that I'm completely over it, this has been a suc-
cessful catharsis, and I'm ready to move on...sorry.

[*Audience cheers. Again. Louder this time.*]

                    ANITA LIBERTY (cont'd.)
I call this poem "Alone At The Top."

I'm rich and famous.
I want for nothing,
because I have it all.

Jealous?
You should be.
That's why I am where I am.
To make you feel bad about yourself
and how little you've accomplished.
To make you realize the fact that you haven't
realized your potential.

I have a cool life now.
Everything is within reach
and someone else reaches for it and hands it to me
so I don't have to strain myself.
I live this life to spite you, despite you,
in spite of you.
And now you're just a face in the crowd of upturned
faces pointed in my direction.
Because you see me now and know that you fucked up.
How does that feel?
That was my only goal.
To make you regret your decision to leave.

144

You are not forgiven.
You are not forgotten.
You are not for me.
See ya. Wouldn't want to be ya.

[*The audience sits in hushed awe for a moment,
absorbing the magnitude and symmetry of Anita
Liberty's latest creation and then, as if signaled
by a higher power, they start clapping in celebra-
tion and jubilation. She has changed their lives
and they are grateful.*]

I would like to take all the credit for making this book happen.

But that wouldn't be right.

And because I like to do what's right…
here's commendation and many heartfelt thanks to:

First and foremost, Peter Borland, because he's supportive and smart and cute. (Good qualities to have in an editor.)

Patty Brown of John Boswell & Associates, who approached selling this book like she was doing the publishing world a favor. (My kind of approach.)

Cindy Schultzel of Howard Entertainment for doing an amazing job managing this sometimes-unmanageable girl.

Michelle Ferrari, Janice Maloney, Deborah Brody, Victorria Johnson, Laura Weinstein, Sally Davies and Michael Calleia who, each in their own distinct and specific (and, in Michelle's case, frequently emphatic) ways, directly contributed to the body of work that makes up this book.

Elizabeth Cashour and Steven Saden of Zipper, and Tim Maner and Kristin Marting of HERE, who always knew when to give me space. (To do my show.)

Sam Bisbee, Toby Blue, Amy Brenneman, Christopher Duva, Emily Grayson, Neeltje Henneman, Scott Howard, Christopher Liam Moore, Nancy Rose, Linda Reitzes, Brad Silberling and Susan Sterman for offering many examples of their support of me. Oh, and of my work.

And, finally, my family (Idelle, Julian, Todd, Phoebe and Beau) for making me into the person (or people) I am today.

147

About the Author

Anita Liberty performed her first one-woman show, "Not Thinking About You," at HBO's U.S. Comedy Arts Festival in Aspen in 1996. Her weekly episodic Web site, "Give Me Liberty," launched in 1997 as HBO's inaugural Web-based comedy program. *Anita Liberty* (a short film) was shown at the 1997 Sundance Film Festival and had its television premiere on the Independent Film Channel on Valentine's Day, 1997.

Anita Liberty is a character created and performed by Suzanne Weber.

NOTES:

NOTES:

NOTES:

NOTES:

NOTES:

not thinking about you.

— Anita **Liberty**

still not thinking about you.

— Anita **Liberty**

If you received this postcard, you should go out right now and buy the Ballantine book HOW TO HEAL THE HURT BY HATING by Anita Liberty. Go on! It's in bookstores across the country. Just waiting to be bought. By you. And every single one of your friends.

to

_____

_____

_____

_____

So? Have you gone out yet and bought your copy of the Ballantine book HOW TO HEAL THE HURT BY HATING by Anita Liberty? It's in bookstores all over the country and it has your name on it. Well, it could have your name on it. If you buy it and then put your name on it. Be my guest. Once you've bought it, you can put your name all over it for all I care. Have a ball.

to

_____

_____

_____

_____